DID YOU SING YOUR SONG?

MARY C. EARLE

Did You Sing Your Song?: Poems

Published by Material Medial LLC
5150 Broadway #466
San Antonio, TX 78209
www.MaterialMedia.com

To contact Material Media directly within the US, please use email:
Info@MaterialMedia.com.
Non-profits or bulk orders: Elizabeth@MaterialMedia.com

Publisher's Cataloging-in-Publication Data
Names: Earle, Mary C, 1948-, author.
Title: Did you sing your song? : poems / Mary C. Earle.
Description: San Antonio, TX: New Beginnings, An Imprint of
Material Media, 2020.
Identifiers: LCCN 2019947235 | ISBN 9781947460072 (pbk.) |
9781947460140 (ebook)
Subjects: LCSH Poetry, American. | BISAC Poetry / American / Genera
Classification: LCC PS3605.A753 D6 2020 | DDC 811.6--dc23

Design by Andréa Caillouet
Cover illustration by Laura Lopez
Printed in the United States of America

For my mother, Mary Kopecky Colbert,
who taught me to love poetry

CONTENTS

PART 2: VOICES FROM SCRIPTURE

PART 3: PILGRIMAGES

INTRODUCTION

I grew up listening to song. My parents and grandparents sang to me from the time I was born. Perhaps because of that sweet exchange, when I was around two or three, I sensed a deeper song, a melody that could be perceived in wind and rain, in trees and flowers. I also had an awareness of a hum that sounded through everything—just beyond the reach of my range of hearing. The hum could be felt, like feeling the beat of a drum in the floor of a dancehall.

I am a child of San Antonio and the Texas hill country. I grew up being able to roam Olmos Creek with my sister, scrabbling up and down cliffs, watching for grass snakes and spiders. We rode our bikes far and wide, visiting the creek and parks that were within several miles of our house. We chose to be outside, to relish the sounds of crickets and songbirds.

Almost every weekend, we went out to the land my maternal grandparents, Joe and Golda Kopecky, owned outside of Boerne, TX. We had no running water at "the ranch." We used an outhouse. We were given free reign of the 200 acres. We both remember well the movement of the cedar trees when a new cold front blew in, and the singular song of the branches. The creek had it's own melody, which changed if there had been a big rain. We learned over time to distinguish the sounds of deer in the brush, armadillos in the leaves, coyotes on the cliffs.

So much of my young life was spent cheek by jowl with hill country rock and fossil. That landscape shows up in reverie and in dreams. The songs of that habitat sing in my cells.

That ancient hum was complemented by poetry. My mother, Mary Kopecky Colbert, loved language. She read continually and widely. When my sister Susie and I were young, Mom read A.A. Milne poems to us. To this day, we can recite "James, James/ Morrison, Morrison/ Weatherby George Dupree/ took great care/ of his Mother/ though he was only three." When we were older, Mom introduced us to the poetry of Robert Service. She leaned toward lyric poetry that told a story. She loved the sound of the words, and her delight in reciting was contagious.

When I was in the third grade, my teacher, Miss Pat Hartman, invited us students to try our hand at writing poetry. I still remember writing that poem about my grandmother, and then reading it to her. It had an internal rhyme scheme. How I knew about that in the third grade remains a mystery.

Over time, I learned to speak Spanish and majored in Spanish in college. I lived in Mexico for a time doing graduate studies, and my husband Doug and I lived there during the first year of marriage. To this day, sometimes I dream in Spanish. Occasionally, I will be speaking and be unable to retrieve the English translation of a Spanish word I just used. So, these poems have some mix of Spanish and English. I am, after all, born and bred in a bilingual, bicultural city. My mother's family went to Mexico City in the summers in the 1930s so that my grandfather could teach medicine and cardiology at the Universidad Nacional Autónoma de México. As a consequence, I grew up listening to stories in both English and Spanish.

As an Episcopal priest, my own language for prayer and poetry is indelibly shaped by *The Book of Common Prayer.* Both syntax and vocabulary are influenced by a life long use of that beloved resource, as well as the hymns we use in worship. I "caught" the joy of liturgical music and song from my father, Gene Colbert. When I sat next to him during Morning Prayer, I would lean against his chest to hear and feel the vibrations as he sang, "Come let us sing unto the Lord." Dad wasn't a great singer; he was often off-key. Yet the direct simplicity of his devotion came through, almost like a transfusion, from his chest to my ear.

In my ongoing life of study and teaching, I've been influenced strongly by the Christian desert tradition, Celtic spirituality, the Benedictine Rule and Julian of Norwich. I've written books on these subjects, taught classes and led retreats focused on this material. I'm formed by a long established habit of reading and praying scripture. Narratives from the New Testament live in my imagination and in my heart; they shape me and the way I pray.

Lastly, through the writing of the Irish poet and theologian John O'Donohue, I discovered the Irish notion of *oran mor,* which refers to the deep, eternal Song. This tradition holds that the Divine Source sings everything into being, at every moment, in every breath. Our invitation and joy is to listen for that everliving Song, and to join ourselves to it. I have begun to regard all of my writing, teaching, and leading of retreats as verses in that magnificent Song, not always on key, never perfect, yet full of the desire to join in the melody that flows through the universe and brings forth abundant life.

The poems in this collection have been written over the last 20 years. Some are fairly new. Some have been published in journals or anthologies. In the summer of 2018, I realized that the eternal Song that sings everything into being was inviting me to gather the poems together, and offer them to you, the reader. May they lead you to sing your own song.

Part One: Land

KENDALL COUNTY, TEXAS

Almost every weekend,
I'd get in the backseat of Grandma Golda's Chevy,
anticipating that escape and homing.

The creek was my mother.

Along her banks I befriended turtles
and gave water moccasins their due.
I learned to still body and soul—
striped bass, my teacher,
fins barely moving
to the unheard hymn of the creek.

I plucked fossils out of caliche
as if they were ancient fruit,
ripe for the taking.

I hosted my share of chiggers and ticks.

I watched sky and shadow,
cedar limbs and light.
As seasons changed,
as dark became light,
as north wind called the trees
to bow down and worship.
Cypress bough overhead,
gilded frog's music,

turkey-gobble chant at day's end—
a vast and varied chorus
warbling, chirping, bellowing, hissing:
"Holy, holy, holy."

LATECOMER

When I step on this limestone
my foot searches for the feet of ancestors.
The fossil fronds and bivalves tell me:
Life has unfolded here for eons.

I am a latecomer.

I want to be gathered into the circle
of those who have gone before—
so I lug the stones, make a circle,
light a fire.

Then I ask each ancestor to take a seat,
to tell me what their eyes have seen,
to give me the age-old chant
that these rocks
yearn to hear again.

EARTH HUNGER

Tengo hambre.
The hunger that makes my gut ache.
Ando hambrienta, buscando la tierra
que me cuida, que me nutre.
Tierra negra, tierra roja, tierra amarilla.
Tierra de alma, tierra madre, madre tierra.
Tierra.

NEW FOOTING

"Ven aquí m'hija," She whispers.
"Mira, look at these stars
between your toes.

Stop that whining!

No llores, no. Ya, ya. Mira, tus deditos,
Look how pretty those feet are—
covered with petals,
covered with *estrellitas."*

Star-toes, feet adorned with the heavens.

And me, little-girl proud,
seeing my feet as She does,
seeing twinkle toes on this body broken,
seeing heaven beneath my feet.

FOOTPRINTS

Walking the creekbed,
looking for fossils and arrowheads,
other evidence of Your tracks on earth,
I am reminded of Bonaventure.
He too tracked You in nature.
He found Your footprints in the dirt, in the forest,
in the rock.

You have been playing with atoms
for a long, long time.
These eons old shells and hot pink flints
tell us that You have left us hints.

Why paint the flint pink or midnight blue?
Why scatter these aged shells along deer paths?
"Follow the footprints," my friend Bonaventure says.
Follow the clues.
Follow the trail divinity leaves
like some exuberant child
dribbling finger paint
and working with clay.

MI TIERRA

I am not Mexican by blood
yet this is *mi tierra.*
Es la tierra de mi carne y hueso.
It's the earth that gave rise to sinews and nerves
stretching across this skeletal frame.

Esta tierra es mía,
y yo soy de esta tierra.

Querida tierra,
I am in you and you are in me:
Mutual indwelling
of cedar brake and flesh,
hard scrabble and gut.

I've grown roots here,
roots so long and deep
that no amount of cedar-chopping
will dislodge me from this soil.

OBITUARY

When I lie down that last time
upon the folds of hill country earth,
I want to hear the cypress lullaby
as my bones let go.

I want cardinal praise, red and raucous,
filling the air
as my dust returns to dust.

I want the breeze that whistles down the creek bank
to gather up my ashes in its eternal song,
to gather and cast in one sweet movement,
scattering those atoms that were briefly mine,
into the soil as old as the hills.

TO THE CHAMA RIVER VALLEY

I want to lie down
on your rocky hillside
and pull your dark skin up over my body
like one of my grandmother's quilts.

I want to snuggle down
with the worms and the beetles
laying my flesh on your flesh,
skin to skin,
listening with a child's hopeful heart
for an ancient lullaby,
an even older rocking sway,
a tender whisper,
a kiss goodnight.

THREE TIMES DAILY

Grind two cups of limestone outcroppings.
Add water from Grape Creek.
Make me a poultice.
Apply it warm.

Distill a tincture of bluebonnet and sage.
Take care with the essence.
Give me a tablespoon three times daily.

Grind up cedar berries, mesquite leaves and
prickly pear.
Add to a warm bath.
Let me soak.

This hill country *curandera*
binds up bruises,
sings wild bird chant,
rocking gently while the earth hums.

MATERNAL LINEAGE

Only recently have I come to know
this female lineage on my Daddy's side:
Leary, which means "kingdom of the sea."

Great Grandma Anna was of that tribe of
Irish-born seers.
She stares out from a photograph,
ram-rod straight,
her will strong enough
to bend her offsprings' lives to suit her,
strong enough to make Aunt Mattie
never leave her side.

She died at 93, in her cold bed
in that old house in Alexandria, Louisiana.

Lost to me are her stories,
her links to the tribe from County Cork,
her mother's mother's memories
of that green, green land.

I come from the Kingdom of the Sea,
from that watery domain
where otters and sea urchins are at home,
where mermaid's voices sing all but forgotten music.

JARDÍN

Look at that pink.
Rosa fuerte, 'manita!
And the yellow!
AY—to die for!
Pónme a little of the deep blue
and maybe some white for accents.

She whispers to me, *mi jardín.*
Me habla en español.
Siempre quiere que la acaricie con cariño,
que la vista de colores.
Es muy celosa,
pero como una fiera.

We make love every afternoon,
a la hora de siesta.
And I have the scratches to prove it.

TOMATOES ON THE FEAST OF ST. MICHAEL

The plants had gotten that woody, stressed look,
the look that pleads for uprooting, for composting.
The last tomatoes had tasted of mush and exhaustion.

Then we had rain—glorious showers and cooler nights.
Today, on the Feast of St. Michael,
the new green of fruit forming
greets me in the garden.
The new green of spring, here, now,
in the ebbing days of September.

The new green gleams on orbs of forming flesh,
on branches dulled by summer's heat,
amid leaves curled yellow, drying day by day.

"Behold: I make all things new," echoes in my heart
as I touch the baby green flesh
of spring manifesting in autumn.

NIGHT WATCH

Barred owl eyes
scan the dark,
feathers unmoving,
body still.

Knowing through sight and sound—
minute vibration that runs in blood and spirit.

Knowing when to watch, when to wait in utter
stillness.
When to spread your wings,
when to launch,
when to soar.

You read the landscape and
pray the evening office—
your prayer stall a utility pole.

Alert watcher:
Holy one.
Pray for me now and at the hour of my death.

GRAPE CREEK AT TWILIGHT

Striped bass glide to silent music.
Cypress boughs await the wind's invitation
to swing dance.
A gilded frog, haloed by sun-streamed water
blinks as the evening chant begins:
Chirps, ribbets, trills.
Day ends.
Turkeys offer compline.

CICADA COMING OUT

She looked dead.
Though her new spring-green wings
were fully extended,
she lay on her back with the shell of her old life—
her cicada carcass—
on top of her belly.

I felt sad and apprehensive.
Coming out is such hard work,
and on occasion
we damn near expire from the effort.

Then later I spied her on her back still,
newly freed appendages wiggling, perhaps gleeful.
Freedom! Freedom!

I extended my pen.
She grabbed tight and righted,
that new vulnerable body,
still wondering at this incarnation,
discovering what wing, limb and belly
are in bright green.

Now she's resting,
gathering strength.
Like any newborn,
she's taking in the startling reality
of emerging yet again.

FISH

What does the fish know?
The underwater perspective
is something I've always desired.

The knowing that comes
from hiding in the rock crevice,
watching the surface for evidence of dinner.

The flash of movement,
resulting in a gulp,
swallowing whole a wiggling fly.
What does it feel like, that tickle in the gullet?
What does the fish know, swallowing life whole?

DROUGHT BREAKING IN AUGUST

The rain has begun again,
gentle as soft tears.
Droplets dimple the creek.
The cardinal demands more food.

Appetite awakened,
he loves to eat in the rain.

NORTHER

The air hangs like musty old drapes,
hangs heavy, almost paisleyed with dust
and the tired miasma of summer's heat.

Was the movement real or just imagined?
Did the topmost leaves of that old pecan tree
stretch heavenward, yearning for moisture,
yearning for promise?

Now they begin a prancing little dance,
wind-driven, whirling a bit,
while lower branches wonder
what the fuss is all about.

Those heavier limbs must be a little cynical.
It is, after all, only the first week of September.
And yet the quickening continues.
The dance picks up and begins to look
more and more like Russian Cossacks
whirling around in crazed circles,
joy gone wild
dervishes set loose upon the world,
dervishes of cold gusts, lightning limned.

The tree stretches, rouses, hopes.
Then rain comes in heavy blue sheets,
sashing, pouring, soaking as summer heat breaks.

FROGS

Felt before heard.
Throaty voices:
amphibian chorus
giving voice to joy.

Water comes in the desert.

EROS

Fingers sinking deep in dirt,
I make the hollow.
The "Surefire" tomato finds her niche.

"Plant it deep," the fellow said.
"All the way up to the first real branching.
That way there will be lots of roots,
lots of roots to withstand the extremes of Texas."

I feel as if I am covering bone of my bone,
flesh of my flesh.
Such a peculiar tenderness in placing the plant just so,
gently patting soft mounds, blanketing the roots.

Tomato scent rises like incense.
Prayer springs from this simple act—
stooping down to earth,
touching that loamy soil that at the end
will receive me with enfolding care.

GREENING WEB

For St. Hildegard of Bingen and Dylan Thomas

Greening pulse of earth—
That surge binds all:
"The One who made thee
made me likewise."

The web throbs with the greening power of God—
the web woven by Wisdom herself,
carefully, kindly linking
rocky crevice and swampy shore,
cicada's wing and badger's tooth,
woman's belly and man's thigh.

The greening web knits wheat to grape,
purls chile to corn.
Every moment the design emerges,
and here we are,
knit together in our Mother's womb.

ADVENT INTIMATIONS

Flash of fin in a curling wave.
Whirr of feathers in the ancient oak.
Glint of moon shadows patterning the grass.
Heaps and humps of tunneled earth.
Ripples and flutters in a quickening womb.
Hints. Suggestions. Glimmerings.

Keep watch.

SWAN SONG

I know now that I was never a duck.
Ugly I became,
taking in their mirroring,
becoming the ugliness they perceived.
I know now that I never was a duck.

The plumage that I bore in those younger years
was mine alone;
elegant feathers now sprout
where supposed duck down
cloaked this flesh.

And this neck!
No duck has my varied perspectives—
looking down from above,
then up from underneath the water,
peering through roots and fish,
seeing from both sides now.

MADRE ÁRBOL ME PLATICA or WHEN THE TREE SAYS SOMETHING

Oye. Listen up. Pay attention.
Sit still.
Find your center.
Look at me.
Look close, look long, look with care.

Have I not been torn?
Have I not been sundered by lightning?
Yes, I am marked forever.

Yet I continue.

I keep going.
I am not dead yet.
And neither are you.

MADRE ÁRBOL ME PLATICA or WHEN THE TREE SAYS SOMETHING 2

Sit. Look.
Be still.
Go deep.
Feel your roots.
Your roots will feed you.
Your roots will draw up the juice.

Hush. *Cállate.*
I'm talking.
I am only going to say this once.

Being a tree is being a tree.
It's that simple.

Be you.
Trust your roots to connect you.
Trust your roots to feed you.
Trust.
Ahí está todo.

HER HOLY VOICE

Her rivering sound speaks,
those liquid sibilants mixed
with vowels long and open.
Flowing language whose inherent syntax
names the mercurial light in stone,
coaxes us to peer in,
to see this green world
light charged.
Punctuation of bank and tree
shape this water tongue—
an oral tradition
still speaking in my dreams.

COUNTRY LOVE

When I was little I fell in love.
Not just puppy love, mind you,
but wild, ecstatic, crazy love.

I fell in love with rocks, fossils, cedars, creeks,
armadillos, hawks and deer.
I fell in love with this particular earth.

My heart has never left,
and whenever I return and wander over rocky soil,
watching for a glimpse of white-tail,
keeping an eye out for a copperhead,
I am healed.

What was torn and weary,
raggedy-as-all-get-out,
receives the kindly balm of this landscape
I call home.

Part Two:
Voices from Scripture

HANNAH'S COUNSEL

As she continued praying before the LORD, Eli observed her mouth. Hannah was praying silently; only her lips moved, but her voice was not heard; therefore Eli thought she was drunk. So Eli said to her,

'How long will you make a drunken spectacle of yourself? Put away your wine.' But Hannah answered, 'No, my lord, I am a woman deeply troubled; I have drunk neither wine nor strong drink, but I have been pouring out my soul before the LORD.
—I SAMUEL 1:12-15

Hannah came to me this morning
on this Feast of the Visitation,
touching my face
with her papery dark hands,
saying, "Sure, little sister,
sure you are vexed.
Pour that out.
Pour that out—
the libation of hurt and betrayal.
Yes, they will think you're drunk.
But who the hell cares.

I tell you this:
Out of the vexation—
this prayer of sighs and tears,
a rant with jagged edges
and no fine crafted images—
out of this raw and bloody mess,
something new can happen.
So pour it out, little sister.
Pour it all out."

ANNA THE PROPHETESS

There was also a prophet, Anna the daughter of Phanuel, of the tribe of Asher. She was of great age, having lived with her husband seven years after her marriage, then as a widow to the age of eighty-four. She never left the temple but worshiped there with fasting and prayer night and day. At that moment she came, and began to praise God and to speak about the child to all who were looking for the redemption of Jerusalem.

—LUKE 2:36-38

Eighty-four years I've been living.
No small feat.
Days filled with prayer,
with sitting still, hoping to glimpse
something, anything new.

It's harder now.
The cataracts dull my vision.
I peer through a veil.

It was when I turned that I sensed it.
Can't say I saw it—
More like a knowing.

She turned.
I had this chill going
up and down my spine.
That baby, cradled by his teenage mother—
she probably hasn't got
a lick of sense.
That baby.

How like You, Old Holy One,
to come to me in disguise.

How like you to almost sneak past me
after all these years of waiting.
How like you to show up now
when my eyes are so cloudy
I can't make out his face.

THE ANOINTING WOMAN

And a woman in the city, who was a sinner, having learned that he was eating in the Pharisee's house, brought an alabaster jar of ointment. She stood behind him at his feet, weeping, and began to bathe his feet with her tears and to dry them with her hair. Then she continued kissing his feet and anointing them with the ointment.

—LUKE 7:37-38

I came into that room
with the glass jar full,
the jar
glinting in light from the doorway.

I sought that face,
those eyes,
my body taut
with gratitude and the aching
need to touch this man who
had touched me.

Alert,
I heard that voice
laughing,
chortles rolling up from that belly,
chuckles erupting from way down deep.

I heard that voice,
moved towards him,
shaking.

Tears, gushing tears.

Then I was on my knees.

I am no seer.
I am just one of those women
who loved too much.
Yet I knew in a second,
in one brief flash of knowing,
that his path of life
would lead to death.
We always do that, you know.
We kill goodness.
Something in us still
wants to drown the kitten,
rape the child,
tear the wings off the butterfly.

I kissed those feet,
Kissed the toes that walked
from Jericho to Jerusalem.
Kissed the soles
that walked with me.
Kissed the bony arch
and saw the tender place
that a nail would soon tear open.

At night now
I sometimes feel that road-weary flesh against my lips.
I remember the smell of dust and sweat.
I remember that his feet looked a lot like mine.
I remember this: he loved those kisses.

My tears made little
watery tracks down his toes.
His hand reached
out and caressed my hair,
my long dark hair,
that fell like a curtain,
veiling my kisses
in the half-lit room,
veiling this sweet exchange
of our desert
darkened
skin.

MEDITATION 2, THE ANOINTING WOMAN

—LUKE 7:37-38

Yes, I'd been forgiven much,
but not like you think.
Maybe I slept around some,
but you know what?
That isn't what bothered him.
It was what I was doing to me.
He's not a puritan, thank you Jesus.
He isn't hung up on the sex thing.
What he said to me was this:
Do no harm to yourself.

Well, hell.
When was the last time
anyone even saw there was a 'me' to consider?
When was the last time
someone looked my way
and saw ME,
looking out from these eyes,
peering out on the world,
wondering when
there would be a time
for me.

Then he comes up
and says, "Don't hurt yourself."
All of a sudden
it
hit
me.

By God,
I am not
nothing.
By God,
there's something,
someone,
here worth caring for,
worth protecting,
worth handling with respect.

That's what he forgave.
My not knowing,
my not remembering
who I am.

And here's what he blesses:
My standing up with sass and class,
looking you in the eye
and expecting
you are going
to look
back.

SOMEBODY'S GOT TO TELL HIM
MEDITATION 3, THE ANOINTING WOMAN

—LUKE 7:37-38

Peter and the others, they don't see.
They sit around telling jokes, horsing around.
Maybe they do see, but they don't want to know.
Maybe they do see, and they don't know what to do.

Here's what I see, these eyes of mine,
looking out, taking in—
The way he looks off from time to time,
like he gets lost in some deep scary cave,
the way when he thinks no one is looking
he gets all wistful and tender.

You can tell he sees it coming.
You can tell he knows something big is coming down.
One thing I can't stand is all this acting
like nothing is going on.

So I got that oil.
I got that oil and I went to their fraternity supper
and I knelt down.
I broke that bottle open just like my heart.
I cried all over those feet.
I cried and I kissed.

I kissed and I touched.
Somebody's got to stand with him.

Somebody's got to let him know
we can do more than do small talk.
Somebody's got to kneel down here at those feet
and let him know we see what's coming.

So I got that oil and I knelt down
and even though my throat was all tight and
small with tears,
my hands could say, "I know."
My hands could say, "I love you
and I'm scared for you
and I'm missing you already."

My hands could touch that fear
lurking in his limbs
and my hands could hold that fear for a little while.
My hands could say, "I'm here. I'm here."

ELIZABETH DREAMING

Now Abraham and Sarah were old, advanced in age; it had ceased to be with Sarah after the manner of women. So Sarah laughed to herself, saying, 'After I have grown old, and my husband is old, shall I have pleasure?'

—GENESIS 18:11-12,

After those days his wife Elizabeth conceived, and for five months she remained in seclusion.

—LUKE 1:24

Sarah comes to me at night.
She comes as midwife and friend.
We laugh about our old husbands,
and I tell her what only she could understand.
I tell her of sagging breasts now swelled with milk,
of a wrinkled belly now growing round,
of movement inside me,
unpredictable flutters and thumps,
rippling waves
beneath that skin.

ANNUNCIATION

The angel said to her, 'Do not be afraid, Mary, for you have found favor with God. And now, you will conceive in your womb and bear a son, and you will name him Jesus.

—LUKE 1:30-31

I did say "yes"
but not the way you think—
Not with adoring dog-like eyes
cast upwards awaiting a swoon.
I said "yes," after we had a heart-to-heart,
Gabriel and I—him all shiny-winged
and checking out his brilliance in the mirror.

He showed up,
scared me half to death.
He showed up with
what he thinks is good news.

I asked him when was the last time he had a baby.
When was the last time
he felt the sour taste in his mouth,
when was the last time he lived on soda crackers.
I asked him when was the last time
he tried to get some sleep with a bladder that has
nowhere to go.
I asked him:
Do you know what you are asking me?

He didn't and neither did God.
Neither one gets it from my side of things.
But then I figured,
if this is God's son,
he can get it from the inside out.

So I did say "yes"
as long as Gabriel and God understood one thing—
my carrying this baby
meant they had to be pregnant too.

DINAH

Now Dinah the daughter of Leah, whom she had borne to Jacob, went out to visit the women of the region. When Shechem son of Hamor the Hivitie, prince of the region, saw her, he seized her and lay with her by force.

—GENESIS 34:1-2

You say I
have no voice;
you say I
did not speak.

It is you who
do not listen.
It is you who
will not hear.

Hush. Listen to this
flesh of mine, screaming
in the night, terrified
and raw,
opened before her time.

Listen to the blood
rushing like a stampede,
the crimson wanting to burst through
my very pores,
spilling out
the unwanted fluids
washing out every drop of him.

You do not listen.
You do not want to know.

My body speaks her own language,
each sinew and ligament sounding,
echoing down the centuries:
NO.
NO.
NO.

ME AND PETER

Simon Peter answered him, 'Lord, to whom can we go? You have the words of eternal life. We have come to believe and know that you are the Holy One of God.'

—JOHN 6:68-69

To whom else shall I go?

I tried knocking on other doors.
Even when opened, they do not open out.
Even when I am invited in,
the space does not welcome.

And so I go again to You,
heart in hand,
heart fixed, yet also wounded,
heart aroused,
yet also beseeching.

To you I go,
heart in hand,
offering what I have—
what You have made,
wondering if this flesh,
which sure isn't what it used to be,
might still be desirable,
to You who came to me.

THE WOMAN WITH THE ISSUE OF BLOOD

Now there was a woman who had been suffering from hemorrhages for twelve years. She had endured much under many physicians, and had spent all that she had; and she was no better, but rather grew worse. She had heard about Jesus, and came up behind him in the crowd and touched his cloak, for she said, 'If I but touch his clothes, I will be made well.' Immediately her hemorrhage stopped, and she felt in her body that she was healed of her disease.

—MK. 5:25-34

Dear sister,
What was the disease
that kindled
the fire of risk
that burned along your bones,
licking at cells
grown sad
and stagnant with despair?

Bleeding does that—
drains away energy, strength, hope, life.
Bleeding day after day,
month after month,
year after year,
watching life-blood flow out,
watching yourself erode.

A quickening came before
what fringe met your outstretched fingers.
A quickening came within you,
a kindling of the fire of life,
leaping up, sparking,
in a shimmering arc
leading you to the life giver.

The One at your center
broke open your deepest desire,
set you free,
led you who had been long untouched
to stretch out,
seek that fringe—
the fringe where life dwells
the fringe where
risk comes down to this:
stretching reaching,
by hope and with hope and in hope.

THE WOMAN BENT

And just then there appeared a woman with a spirit that had crippled her for eighteen years. She was bent over and was quite unable to stand up straight. When Jesus saw her, he called her over and said, 'Woman, you are set free from your ailment.' When he laid his hands on her, immediately she stood up straight and began praising God.

—LUKE 13:11-14

My back has hurt for 18 years.
Or is it eighteen thousand?
My back has all but given out.
I have looked down day after day,
looked at my feet, looked at the dirt,
looked at these toenails lined with grime
and the calluses now hard as horn.
I have looked down
for I could not look up.

I have been bent for so long
I thought this was how I was made.
I have been bent for so long
I thought this was how I was created.
I'd forgotten what it was to stand straight.

I'd forgotten how this body felt
when the vertebrae stack one upon another,
nice and straight.
I'd forgotten what it was like to breathe in
and feel that good air rush through
heart, gut, lungs.
I'd forgotten what things look like if I stand up.

I had been so used to being bent
that being straight feels odd.
Feels like new shoes.
Feels like I'm a different person.
Feels like I can see, breathe, move, speak.
Feels like I can't be bent again.
Feels like I am a different woman, and yet this body
knows that being bent is hell.

Funny thing, when He laid hands on me,
He felt my spine.
Felt those bumps
that others flinch from.
Felt those protrusions.
Funny thing, when He laid hands on me,
I wanted to stand up.
Something in me remembered—
I have not always been curved and twisted.

So now I can breathe,
I can take a breath and simply feel the rush of air.
I can see the sky.
I can look those bastards in the eye.
I can speak because I can breathe.
And I have plenty to say.

The dirt taught me a lot, you see.
I spent so long looking at that dust between my toes
that I know some things.
I made friends with soil,
with grime,
with earth.
I made the acquaintance of the dust they abhor.
And she is my friend.
That dust will not let me go.
Now when I bend over to see her,
it is out of love and memory.
It is out of wanting to remember being bent,
so that I do not bend another.
It is out of wanting to receive whatever gifts
being bent gave me.

I had been bent so long,
that woman is a part of me.
She learned some things
in that distorted posture,
She knows.

So now, when I stand straight,
when those vertebrae stack gently one by one,
when the stretching of limb and ligament
frees this body of those age-old contortions
I give thanks to the me who was bent—
for seeing it through
for carrying on
for birthing the one
who can stand up straight
and speak.

Part Three:
Pilgrimages

PILGRIMAGES

My pilgrimages
are expeditions
into the hidden bodies of my mothers.

All those names were hidden behind their husbands'.
All those links to my people
were boxed up, closeted away and forgotten.

Now I have names: Leary, McCrary, O'Neill.
Now I have roots like a live oak's.
Now I have some inkling
about why the step dance moves me so,
and why I prefer to look west from rocky coastal cliffs.

These mothers have been calling me for years,
disturbing my sleep,
stirring in my blood,
ready to burst with story and song
just waiting for me to remember.

FOOTNOTES

Where are my mothers?
Where are all those women
whose prayers have woven
the delicate tatting,
the intricate lacework
that holds everything together?

After an eternity of searching,
I began to catch a flutter,
a flash in the darkness,
a movement in the fog.

They are there, hidden in the footnotes.
In the footnotes to the footnotes.
In the unedited manuscripts
slowly mildewing in convent vaults.
Their words still speak from fading ink.
They clamor to be heard.

No longer willing to be hushed,
they storm my library,
pushing books off the shelves,
opening to the back and
pointing to the small print.
"Look!" they insist.
"We are right here waiting."

FOLLOWING FEET

I followed my feet in Ireland,
followed these soles,
tingling with sacred presence.
Inishmore. Clonmacnoise. Ardfert.

I followed my feet, not my head.
Not my heart. Not my gut.

Those feet knew they were on holy ground.
Pin needle sensations traveled up the nerves
of my legs.
My feet told me: the land was made of bone and ash.
This is the dirt that enfolded my great grandmother.

That soil held my feet,
grabbed my toes, pleaded with me to stay,
to lie down,
to know that clay as home.

GRANDMOTHERS

How many of you are there?

I knew, of course, about Golda and Beth.
What an odd pair of grandmothers they were.
And, of course, about Great Grandma Kopecky—
her Czech peasant build, low and strong.

Now the great great grandmothers come
tumbling forth,
Their presence long sensed, then known.

They like to come for tea in the afternoon.
So much to tell; they interrupt
and try to speak all at once.
They are about to burst with all those stories.
"Here's who you are.
Here's who you come from.
Let us tell you while you sleep.
Just leave us some tea and cookies.
And for God's sake get Irish Breakfast tea."

The stories are here.
In me.
In this body, waiting to unfold in time.

PISTYLL

A hospice church on the pilgrim route to
Bardsey Island, Wales

I have found what I was looking for,
or I have been found.
These old church stones speak of a Body
that reaches out to those in need.
There, behind the altar, a priestly predecessor of mine
gave holy food to holy people,
so many ill and maimed,
collapsed upon the hillside.

Hands outstretched,
some long lost cousin of mine in Christ
handed on the bread,
through small slits in the stone wall, to waiting,
willing others.

The distribution defied the church wall,
ignored the separation,
the splitting,
the cutting off.

Those slits—
two narrow openings for the life to flow out
into the world,

to those whose hearts and bodies ache with suffering,
to those who have come this far,
looking, searching, scanning the universe
for some small glimpse of mercy,
some small taste of kindness.

The churchyard echoes with sounds of those long ago,
hurting, dying.
All those pilgrims struggling on the way
to Bardsey, to the Isle of 10,000 saints.
And the churchyard is still full
of saintly ministering presences,
calling us to reach through the walls
and distribute the bread.

CLYNNOG FAWR

A church on the pilgrim route to Bardsey Island, Wales

During World War I,
when malevolent gases choked the air,
the vicar of Clynnog Fawr
began again,

began when despair hung heavy,
began when seeing light in the darkness
was almost a lost art.

The vicar of Clynnog Fawr
remembered what had been forgotten.
He awoke from the sleep of centuries,
and called forth those who would walk in the Way.

He called for those who would
use their legs, bodies, minds.

He called for those who would care to sweat and
sacrifice together.
He called for those who would risk remembering what
it is to be a pilgrim,
who would dare to travel with the ones it would be
easier to hate.

He smelled the stench of war,
and that unholy incense went up
as a prayer of beseeching.

When the light was going out,
when the bodies that had been knit together in their mothers' wombs
were bayoneted and dismembered,
the vicar of Clynnog Fawr
called together a pilgrim band to begin again.
In those unholy years in which the last century was born,
the pilgrim walk began anew.

Prayer on foot.
Prayer with bodies.
Prayer together.
Prayer on the way.
Prayer as a company.
Prayer as a promise.

I stand here now before this pilgrim cross.
I am here because he began again.
I am standing with old St. Beuno.
And all the pilgrims old and new.
Soon we will hike Uchmynydd.
Soon we will spy Bardsey Island.

And we will hear and see
the Word that is Light and Life,
the Word that beseeches us,
"For Mercy's sake, will you walk together?
For Mercy's sake, will you walk with me?
For Mercy's sake, will you have mercy?"

ARRIVING IN WALES, SEEKING ST. DAVID

How my eyes are straining,
scanning the clouds for a break,
longing for that first sight of Wales.
All of me, in my eyes,
wanting to see again
that ancient holy ground.

How I love this small country
that has not forgotten the little things,
this place where St. David abides with
every household,
keeping house with the great cloud of witnesses.

SPIRALS

Marking stones heavy with life and death,
holding invertebrate creatures sipping the dew,
spirals eternally etched in fossil remains,
circling stairways in castles and churches.

Spirals of life and death, dying and rising,
womb and tomb,
beginning and ending and beginning again.

How have we forgotten?
How could we have lost this knowing?
In the end is my beginning.
The tomb is a womb.
And in dying we are born to eternal life.

SNOWDON

I feel so small,
and that holds no fear.
I feel as if I am the tiniest one-celled creature
formed in the depths of the sea.
I feel as if I am a grain of sand.
I feel as if I am but one leaf
shimmering on the tallest aspen.

Holy order.

I am a tiny part of the whole.
A living member of the Body.
A creature among a vast and varied family of creatures.

ELEMENTS

Rock, water, earth, sky—
These very atoms are kin to me, kin to you.
When this flesh becomes dust,
I look forward to the reunion,
to the joining again with these elements
that somehow become living bodies.

Rock, water, earth, sky—
Light within sea, life within rock.
Death within life, and life within death.

Rock, water, earth, sky—
The One who made you
made me likewise,
and we are kin, you and I.

STONES

Listen.
The stones speak.
These age old elemental beings
tell of the hand
that drew forth waters.
Hush. Be still.
For pity's sake quiet the chatter.

These stones speak.

ST. MARY'S WELL, ABERDARON, WALES

This water tastes of truth.
This water flows down into body and soul
and sets the captive free.
This water comes welling up clear—
clear as crystal, clear as liquid light.

This water spills forth
from rock older than Methuselah.
This water has been calling me here
from the moment, from the instant,
that I came forth,
dripping and startled, from my mother's womb.

This water, whose Source is as hidden as mine,
this water is my home.

WELL WATER

Sometimes communion looks like bread and wine.
Sometimes communion looks like a bath.
Sometimes communion is wet gladness,
joy dripping from faces lit from within,
by the sheer delight of kindness.

Sometimes communion
is like a splash in the ocean,
like making big steps in wavelets,
sending sparkling drops of wet light
onto faces, hair, eyes.

Sometimes communion comes down to this:
running up a rocky hill
with a plastic bag of well water,
giddy with the abundance of grace
that is tucked away yet flowing
from a crevice as old as God.

ON THE ROAD TO BARDSEY ISLAND

Something new and old flows in me here.
Something as fresh as springs in the rock.
Something as aged as this craggy coast.
Something as elemental
as it was in the beginning.

On the road to Bardsey Island,
I can hear the tromping of pilgrim feet.
I hear the prayers of many,
and I wonder at this holy band,
these saintly presences who walk with us,
telling their stories, urging us to see,
tugging at our hearts and souls
and reminding us that the news is good.

I feel roots sprout from my feet
and leaves bud just below the surface of my skin.
Sap begins to flow within,
coursing through scorched veins,
easing pain and inflammation,
bringing new life so sweet it almost hurts.

THE WELL OF THE WETHERS, COUNTY KERRY, IRELAND

Pilgrims banded by that yearning, that fear,
looking for Presence,
yet not knowing
if we can bear such an in-breaking.

We gather thirsting,
encircling this age-old well
whose waters have washed
many a parched heart.

We hope for elemental simplicity,
a substance that will break all forms,
tenacious as the climbing roses
which fence this space of encounter,
piercing us with beauty.

Peering down, we see our faces mirrored,
mossy green and rippling—

waters that have flowed for centuries,
promising to quicken,
intimating a rippling life within us,

a life that we had all but lost,
stumbling beneath wounds old and new,
guilt bearing down without remorse.

In the Well of the Wethers the waters move,
unseen angels disturb the surface.
We press forward,
mouths already tasting the ancient water of life,
the water from which we emerged,
new and dripping,
so long ago.

RETURN

Once I dreamed I was in a cavern,
swimming in liquid light,
Making like an otter
In water illumined and illuming.

Once I dreamed I was within a sacred cave,
A womb-like space as sacred as mine,
As sacred as my mother's.

Now as I stand on this cliff on Anglesey Island,
Looking west toward Ireland,
The sea dances at my feet,
Water shot through with light—
So inviting I have to restrain the desire
To dive headfirst from this rocky pinnacle
And swim for the depths,
Some ancient melody signing in veins
That have been looking for this moment
Since the world began.

NUESTRA SEÑORA DE LA SALUD, PÁTZCUARO, MICHOACÁN

Beneath the deep blue mantle,
glinting gold,
milagro after milagro, She enfolds and caresses,
hidden fingers promising, healing.

All these tin arms, legs, breasts, hearts.
All these limbs of her body.
All these milagros,
encircling the fear,
encompassing the flesh that fades,
all these milagros beseeching, promising.
All these milagros.

DELIVERANCE

By the River McKenzie where I sat down,
and where I wept
the dainty stars covered my feet,
tugged at my hem, offered tenderness
and delicate petals, hummed soft eternal
lullabies, wiped hard religion's marks
from my face, held me close and
with sweet brave beauty
gentled the anxiety,
guided me away from distant dilemmas,
soothed and caressed,
crooning with Her own dear voice.

LULLABY

When I sit in this field of stars, still,
the distant streaks of light dancing
above my head, the whine of clanking
dogma emptied from my ears.

When I sit still, I find
the forest sings,
a tender nursemaid
cantando en español,
"a la nanita nana,
nanita ella,
nanita ella."
Crooning, soothing, pine
branch caresses, cradles.

When I sit still,
dancing particles of earth, pine and flesh
meet, greet, speak
in words only the wind knows.

CAMPO STELLA

Fields of stars lie under my feet
Here in this campo stella.
Peregrinando vengo. I come
Seeking, searching—*"Entran santos peregrinos, peregrinos."*
"Enter, holy pilgrims. Receive this shelter."
"Reciban este rincón."

I hear her hum,
this distant lub-dub of her
throbbing at her hidden core.

So much for religion, dogma.

Here my body lies down among
the wine colored petals.
Here the stars cover me.
Here I lie down, no need to be brave.
Simply fall down among the stars.

Campo stella/field of stars.
Campo santo/field of souls.

"Ven, m'ija," she whispers,
"reciba este rincón."

THE FRINGE

My heart is not in the heartland.
My center is on the fringe,
on those alluvial borders
of culture, theology, art—
where encounters occur,
others meet, and we are made new.

Where surprise and discovery
are at least possible.
I prefer to venture out to the periphery
and there—
there my heart is firmly fixed.

Part Four: People

GOLDA'S KITCHEN

Long before women's ordination,
Grandma Golda presided in her kitchen,
giving us each a daily bread.

Every day Golda took, blessed, broke, distributed,
just like Jesus, trying to feed a multitude.
No loaves and fishes here,
but still a miracle of plenty.
This crowd of grandkids less than half her height,
hungry for the simple mothering
her offspring could not offer.

Coated with kolache filling, our small hands
held her skirts.
Our noses twitched, as aromas of promise
wafted from her oven.
Cornbread. Yeast rolls. Pecan butter cookies.
Tea cakes. Ladyfingers. And of course, kolaches.
A feast of fat things.

In that kitchen
a little soul's leanness
met the face of abundance,
received a flour printed blessing
marked as Golda's own forever.

ALMOST TO TERM

Her belly is round and taut,
the periwinkle blue of her muu-muu
stretches over the widening orb.
She aches, moans,
places palms on her lower back.

Her world within,
a world of cancer growing, now unchecked,
taking over spleen and liver,
hogging it all,
while strangely suggesting imminent delivery.

JOHNNY

He came in on Sunday morning,
trailing clouds of glory and fumes of booze,
bloated, boo-hooing like a baby,
gold chains dripping on his chest,
calling out for Jesus at the top of his lungs,
whooping and hollering,
kneeling at that altar rail as if it were his—
because somewhere deep down he remembers:
It is.

Somewhere deep down he knows to call that Name,
to speak and expect an answer.

He came bearing gifts
on the 19th Sunday after Pentecost,
crucifixes adorned with gold glitter;
Jesus on the cross, glorified.
Who is this Jesus that Johnny knows?

Johnny.
In all his drunken exuberance,
all his slobbering praise talk,
kneels at the altar in skin tight jogging shorts,
hairy chest exposed to God and man,
shouting for Jesus.

He has the guts of Bartimaeus,
even if the booze has softened his mind.
He still has that desire that takes him to the altar,
pushes him down on his knees,
and sets him to hollering for the Lord.

The crucifix gives me a glimmer:
I bet that when the time comes
and the booze eats his flesh,
old Johnny, drunk and bellowing,
will look up and see the same
glittery glory waiting for him,
opening the arms of mercy and saying,
"Come on home,
come on home."

FOR MY YOUNG FRIEND

Ragged roads cross these slender wrists,
roads red with the price of your own life.

You turn your hands palms up, showing me
the crimson of that night's jagged cry.

The swollen flesh already knits and mends,
as if that self-cleaving were necessary—
the demon escaped, fled your rage,
fled before this stoking sacred fire of NO. NO. NO.

Now you sit still.
So still.
As the holy oil seals these wounds,
the red road of your life gleams,
fire becomes water.
No blood flows here, only tears.

BETTYE

Bettye traveled near and far,
even to Nepal.
She went to see her elephant, her namesake
who resided in the work camp in the jungle.
"She works for her living,"
Bettye said with a laugh.

Bettye traveled near and far,
from despair to contentment,
from health to weakness and back again.
At the end, when the voracious
cells had out-multiplied their host,
she was ready for one more adventure.
She who had packed her bags
for more than one long journey,
got herself together yet again.

She left her flesh to science
in case it could be useful to someone,
just as her clothes went to
the Battered Women's Shelter.

Bettye's ashes finally came home,
long months after her departure,
long months after her last goodbye.

Seeing that mound of dust and bone,
touching the leavings of a life of venturing,

I missed her anew.
Bits of Bettye's lovely bones were in my palm,
the irreducible residue of a life well lived,
a life well traveled,
a life in its own way full and complete.
Those bits of bone were as priceless as gems.
In another age,
I would have been tempted
to create a reliquary.
How she would have laughed!
She was no saint in that pious sweet sense.
She liked her wine
and she could bear one hell of a grudge.

Bettye never forgot the joy of exploring.
Her heart and mind were always ready
for one more jaunt,
one more visit half way around the world.

This is bone of your bone, my friend.
Bone of your bone, still here,
as is our memory of you,
our memory as grand and extraordinary
as that elephant who bears your name
deep in the jungle in India,
half way around the world.

PRIEST OF THE PEOPLE

José can see
by the dawn's early light
that the yanqui has not gone home,
that the yanqui has fed the people
chicken flesh plumped with hormones
too strong for delicate USA palates.

José can see
that the children have breasts.
the breasts of chicken
have grown breasts in children—
children just old enough to read,
now needing B cup bras
thanks to Pfizer and Merck.

José can see,
and because he can,
his eyes flash.
Even the eye that is blind.

His eyes flash,
and his voice speaks.
He says to the yanquis,
"Puerto Rico is not given for you."

ZORRO ON BROADWAY

He strides the sidewalk near Kiddie Park,
Black cape and mask,
revealing and obscuring.

Who is that masked man?

At the bus stop he bows to the ladies,
gestures *con cortesía,*
then, hearing music from another time,
moves in a slow waltz,
his feet remembering that dance
that his grandparents loved.

GOOD FRIDAY IN SAN ANTONIO

Along Broadway, the banners flap and snap,
heralding Fiesta San Antonio
in neon colors.

At San Fernando Cathedral, San Antonians
gather on the vía dolorosa,
walking together as pueblo, as community.
We jostle, weep, talk, wonder,
walking through the story,
shouting, "Crucify! Crucify!"

This fiesta marks us as deeply as the other.
This fiesta marks us as a city still capable
of remembering and being re-membered,
a city still mindful of suffering and lack,
of the little girl on Guadalupe Street
whose eyes glaze from hunger,
of the middle school almost-man
who wants to wear colors and belong,
of the grandmother who has just discovered
the syringe in her grandchild's backpack.

This fiesta of the cross reminds us
that the suffering never stops
nor does the redemption.

WHEN WE SURVEY THAT CROSS

When we survey that wondrous cross.
  May we know You in our own pain
  and in the pain of our enemies.
  May we know You in our own grief
  and in the grief of our enemies.
  May we know You in our despair
  and in the despair of our enemies.
When we survey that wondrous cross.

FRIENDLY ADVICE

¡Cuánto me gusta San Antonio!
I love this city with her gutsy flare.

Just this week at Teka Molino
a woman came through the door,
balancing tacos and salsa,
sipping her tea,
counseling her *amiga:*
"¡Ay pero sometimes you've got to give it
some hip action!"

Ain't it the truth?
Salsa, hip action and friendly advice
just might guide us to the next millennium.

EMILY'S HOPE

Could it be true
that hope is a thing with feathers?
When I sat at Mrs. Durham's feet,
I met Emily's poems face to face.

I found a sister
who seemed to know
something of what it is to despair.
She did not put on the steel magnolia charm,
and bat her eyelashes, pretending feminine
contentment
in the corseted reality of her day.

No.
Her words speak.
And her words sound true.

I, a budding 17 year old,
already felt the cage around
adolescent female growth.

Lesson in mascara for white brows and lashes.
lesson in charm that feels rather like dying:
"This is how women do it."

Emily's words stirred something inside me
that refuses to this day
to be stayed, underwired, girdled or bound.

That thing with feathers
rustles anew.
Hope's feathers begin to move, flutter, fly.

THE TRIBE

"When one is seriously ill," Frances said,
"one enters another reality."

That reality, immense and dark,
enveloped me and kept me safe
despite the gnawing erosion
in my belly.

That reality has never left,
not since that almost fatal falling into the pain.
Now when I re-read Julian of Norwich
and hear of those showings of divine love,
I see that she received them
while at the doorway
between here and there.

I know her as sister,
just as I know Frances as one of the tribe.

We are blood brothers and sisters,
we who have entered that vast space,
who are marked in flesh and blood and spirit.
We are blood sisters and brothers.
we have a secret parlance,
a shorthand,
a silence that says it all.

THE WAITING ROOM

Glossy women smile, shiny teeth showing,
faces adorning Glamour and Vanity Fair.
They offer minimal diversion.
I sit, paging to keep from pacing.
Paging to keep fear from sitting any closer.
Already she's bustled over and
squeezed her ample hips into the seat beside me,
pressed her fleshy forearm against mine,
crowded me against the floral upholstery.

I smell her sharp metallic breath,
hear the way she snaps her teeth,
hold myself still and small,
retreat even further into the chair's recesses,
staring at the model's cover-girl make-up,
satin red lips,
velvet skin,
waiting one more time
in the room where we all wait
in the room where fear takes up every empty seat.

"Move over," I say.
"Go sit across the room."

TRIBAL MARKINGS

For Bill

"I've had a good check-up," you venture,
showing me the purple bruise
hidden in the tender inner crevice of your arm.
Despite the numbers on the lab report,
your eyes question.

That needled flesh, belying yet one more puncture,
speaks your own truth:
something, somewhere, someplace within
is not right.

A few weeks have passed.
Again those tribal marks show.
More blood drawn, more bruising shows.
That distinguishing discoloration of flesh.
You knew even then.

You knew what the lab work did not.
You knew what the tribe knows way down deep.
You knew that the malignancy was on its way back.

SAGES

When I was still
tied down,
punctured,
and doped
an angelic messenger named Celeste (of course)
appeared in the hospital room.
Sparking spirit, bearing flowers,
Celeste left me with a Russian sage's words,
scented with snapdragon and rose:
"The stiller you are,
the farther you will go."

Once home and able to prowl my garden
I discovered that death's dark shadow
had visited the herbs as well.
The basil and oregano lay flattened,
mirroring my own experience:
beat down, ready for compost.
I mourned for days.

Pay attention.
All the sages say that.
Look at what's there.

The bees pointed the obvious out to me.
There, in the garden, next to the herbs that died,
another plant flourished.

Small periwinkle blossoms
buzzed with the honey makers' dance.
So beautiful, I thought.
So connected. Bees and flowers.
Now what is that herb?
Oh, yes.
OH, YES!
Russian sage!
"The stiller you are,
the farther you will go."

ON THE FEAST OF THE EPIPHANY, 1997

We were bumped and blown by a north wind,
blue as my chilled hands.
We gathered to scatter my mother's ashes at church,
shivering with grief, relief and the chill of death.

One by one, we gathered a handful of her ashes.
Dad, my sister, my brothers, me.
On that feast day when divine light is manifest,
and those who are wise journey to see a baby,
tender-new,
wrapped as a gift,
we were scattering ashes.

Even as light came
we were in the valley of the shadow of death.
We stood in that Texas chill,
oak limbs waving frantically above us,
as if to say, "For God's sake, for mercy's sake,
pay attention."

We held Mom's life and death and story,
casting those ashes on holy ground,
then held out hands to living water
that cascaded over numbed fingers,
washing away last bits of dust and reminding us again
of that dying and rising at the heart of it all.

Mute, we stumbled into the church parlor
where someone had lit a fire,
as if to say, "Do not be afraid.
The warmth will return."

A friend brought a chess pie,
one of those southern comfort foods
that our grandmothers made,
though they disagreed about the recipe.

With sugar in our mouths and fire on our backs,
the chill of death receded.
Our blue hands turned pink again.
We watched as icy rain
fell on the ashes and brown grass in the courtyard.

So we celebrated the Epiphany.
The Word was made flesh and dwelt among us.
Light does shine in the darkness.
Even this darkness, the darkness of death and ashes.
The darkness of Mary Kopecky Colbert's end,
and ours, too:
Earth to earth.
Dust to dust.
Ashes to ashes.

Even at the grave,
There is still chess pie
And a fire in the hearth.

ICEFLOW

Creaking and groaning,
caught up in a song
too deep for words,
a primordial sound,
what has been breaks up.

The thaw brings fissures,
cracks that open up possibility.
Floes rub against one another.
Ice creates fire.

Can it be possible that after so long,
after what seems an eternity,
the newness really will come?

The river flows beneath the grey-green ice,
flows unseen, unheard, unnoticed.
The river, currents deep and unplumbed,
warms the glacial frozen surface.
The noise is deafening—
deep waters warm, rise.
South breezes caress the hard as ice surface.

What was breaks up and washes away.
The river is no longer hidden.
Now the deep life is on the surface.

ENTER HOLY PILGRIMS

Entren santos peregrinos! Enter holy pilgrims!
So You greet us as we return home at the end of our earthly days.
Grant us the care and dedication to remember that we will die.
On this our earthly journey, may we be surrounded by pilgrims of this world and the next,
that as we return home, our hearts and souls will readily welcome others:
Entren santos peregrinos! Aquí tienen su casa!
Here is your home!

EVEN AT THE GRAVE, MAGNIFICAT

On the tenth anniversary of my son's death of brain cancer.

"My soul proclaims the greatness of the Lord
and my spirit rejoices in God my savior."
—LUKE 1:46-47

Dear Mother,
Sister,
Friend,
Comadre,
Did you sing your song
as your son cried out,
as thirst convulsed his torn limbs?

Did you sing your song
as the nails pierced
those hands and feet
that you had bathed and kissed?
Did you sing your song
as he breathed his last
and you let him go?
Did you sing your song?

HOMEWARD

When the sadness comes,
as it always does,
I remember that your mantle enfolds him.
I remember that dream: my son in your generous lap,
a lap full of stars,
a lap wide as the night sky.

When the sadness comes,
as it always does,
I remember and I make that turn,
heading homeward to the final reunion.

O COME EMMANUEL

O come, O come Emmanuel
Come now to us, in your many disguises.
Come now to us, in every language.
Come now to us, in every culture.
Come now to us, in every color.
Come now to us, that every moment we breathe may be pregnant with your advent.
Come now to us, that we may breathe and labor and deliver you.
Here, now, in our midst and in our souls.
And let us say: Amen.

RESTORATION

Banging. Hammering. Clanging. Buzzing.
Fascia board weakened by rot
falls away.
In its place, strong new lumber.

This house has needed attention
for longer than I can recall.
Now,
this spring,
as the soft warm light
coaxes toadflax and larkspur from hiding,
as tiny blossoms take
their form on the Italian bush beans,
this house,
my house,
is being made new.

ACKNOWLEDGEMENTS

Chile Verde Review, New Texas, Texas Poetry Calendar, The Windhover, Concho River Review, Here is My Spirit, Women's Uncommon Prayers and Lift Every Voice.

In May 2018, the poet Naomi Shihab Nye spoke at my parish, St. Mark's Episcopal Church in San Antonio. She remarked that poets and writers often receive "unacknowledged invitations" to write and to circulate their work. At that moment, I realized that for several years, Elizabeth Cauthorn, owner of Material Media, had been issuing me a warm invitation to attend to my own poetry, gently nudging me in that direction. I have been writing poetry since elementary school. Some of my poems have been published in anthologies and journals, but I have never gathered selected poems into a small volume.

In July 2018, Steven Purcell, executive director of Laity Lodge in the Texas hill country, offered me the opportunity to stay in Hovde House during creativity week. That time afforded me the gift of solitude, in which I was able to make preliminary selections and begin editing.

My husband Doug gave this project his attention and care, making suggestions about what to leave in, what to leave out. He has encouraged me to honor the poems by taking the step of publishing them, and his steady, gentle support has been invaluable.

Lastly, over the years several poetry teachers have been strong guides and mentors, especially Judith Infante and Carol Coffee Reposa. I'm so grateful for their example and encouragement. I'm also so grateful to those who have heard these poems at readings, and asked that they be published.

—Mary C. Earle